Just Breathe

Discover Slow, Uncomplicated
Time with Jesus

CHRISTINE AGOSTINELLI

WESTBOW
PRESS®
A DIVISION OF THOMAS NELSON
& ZONDERVAN

WestBow Press books may be ordered through booksellers or by contacting:

WestBow Press
A Division of Thomas Nelson & Zondervan
1663 Liberty Drive
Bloomington, IN 47403
www.westbowpress.com
844-714-3454

ISBN: 978-1-6642-8110-3 (sc)
ISBN: 978-1-6642-8111-0 (hc)
ISBN: 978-1-6642-8109-7 (e)

Library of Congress Control Number: 2022919052

Print information available on the last page.

WestBow Press rev. date: 10/25/2022

I humbly dedicate this work to the Holy Spirit. This book would not have been possible without Your steady presence and constant leading in my life–even when I refused to see it. You gently led me back to the open arms of the Father when I had wandered too far and patiently guided me back to the heart of Jesus, where love abounds in endless measure. Surely You have known me, understood me, and have quieted me with Your love. I eagerly share with others the things You have shown me now.

Contents

Call

Focus

Move

Be

Praise for Just Breathe

"This is the most helpful book I've read in a long time because it actually took me somewhere I couldn't get to on my own. Regardless of where you are spiritually—skeptic, doubter, unbeliever, or seasoned follower of Jesus—Christine does a phenomenal job of meeting you there and leading you slowly by hand on a journey that will change your life one simple step at a time." —Sammy Adebiyi, national speaker for Food for the Hungry and lead pastor at Soma City Church

"So many people—Christian and skeptic alike—are living disconnected from God and aren't sure what to do about it (or even if they want to do anything about it). Let Christine be your guide! What does she offer? Honesty, authenticity, experience, wisdom, and simplicity. She not only wrestled with the emptiness of worn-out, complicated, twenty-first-century Christianity, she has penetrated to the beauty and fullness of life with God. I've had a front-row seat to Christine's journey, and I'm convinced her discoveries are desperately needed by many people today. No tired clichés and religious platitudes here; just a life-giving, uncomplicated way of connecting with God that is simple and effective. God invites us into a life of intimacy and connection with Him; He's a relational God and deeply desires for us to come close. But we make it so complicated and difficult. This book will help restore and deepen that longed-for intimacy with God. Whether you feel close to God or distant from Him, Christine's new book will breathe life into your relationship with God as you follow her sage counsel. Read it slow; let it penetrate your soul. I highly recommend this book!" —Dr. Jim Mindling, lead pastor at Church of the Open Door

"Christine Agostinelli will take you deeper in your spiritual journey in an uncomplicated way. This book is like a scuba diving excursion for your soul. Below the surface awaits new self-discoveries, awe-inspiring revelations, and a fresh focus of connecting with Jesus. Put on your soul's wetsuit, prepare your oxygen, dive in, and *breathe!*" —John Paul, educator

"I was very impressed with Christine's heart as I read her words. That is because she really wants the readers to immerse themselves into the powerful thoughts that are presented. Christine causes you to sit and soak and rethink about what the Holy Spirit is saying to you. You will be better for spending the time with this little book because it has big impact on your walk with the Lord." —Dr. Sammie L. Davis-Dyson, author of *My Story for His Glory: The Power of Prayer*

Introduction

I was angry, frustrated, disappointed, and so completely unsatisfied with my experience in the Christian faith. I had doubts and questions welling up inside of me, and I had no idea what to do with them or how to make them go away. A faith that had once felt so easy and so natural now felt so ... *complicated*. I was left feeling isolated and alone, feeling like everyone else had it all figured out while I was the only one struggling. I didn't know how everything had gotten so bad. All I knew is I found myself starving for something I couldn't articulate or explain. The walls of my Christian community that had once felt so safe and so comfortable now felt like they were quickly closing in on me.

Feeling I had no other reasonable option, I decided to leave the Christian faith I had been raised with in search of whatever it was I was so hungry and desperately starving for. Something ... *more*. Something bigger, something better. Something different ... something *else* that could satisfy this growing hunger for more. More of what, I wasn't sure. But I was sure that, whatever it was, I wasn't going to find it in whatever Christianity had to offer. It was then that I left the faith with no plans to ever return.

Walking through that exit door was exhilarating. I felt free and alive for the first time in a very, very long time. In fact, leaving the faith felt like the best decision I could possibly have made. I felt like I was finally free to discover the real me without all the rules of what I should do and the expectations of who I should become. I was excited to see all the wonderful things my new non-Christian future held.

However, after a couple of years of this newly discovered freedom, the novelty and excitement of my decision began to wear off. I still hadn't found what I was longing—*starving*—for. I was still searching and still empty. Everything was more complicated than it ever had been before. I still felt let down by the Christian faith, and now I felt let down by the promise that my life would be better without it. I was more confused than I had ever been.

This went on for a few more years until something strange and completely unexpected began to happen. It had been eight years since I'd left the Christian faith, and now I couldn't deny that something in me was feeling slowly drawn back to it. What happened next, and continues to happen now, is what I aimed to capture in this book. It's a reflection of the slow and uncomplicated process God used to draw my weary, restless, skeptical, prodigal heart back to Him.

It's full of the questions He asked me and the deep truths He showed me. It's full of the promises He revealed to me and, most profoundly, how He showed me the uncomplicated and unhurried way I was meant to connect with Him.

It's the same uncomplicated and unhurried way *you* were made to connect with Him.

No matter where you feel you are in relation to God as you begin—if He feels near or if He feels far—let this book be your guide to help show you how to move your heart closer and closer to the heart of the Father as you work through the pages.

One of the verses that will come up as you go along is James 4:8 (TPT):

"Move your heart closer and closer to God, and He will come even closer to you."

Before you begin, take a few minutes to think about what moving your heart closer to God might look like for you right now. Don't rush; really think about it. Try to picture what that move looks like.

Is it a large bounding leap toward Him?
Is it a sure and confident step or two?
Is it more reserved, like a slow and calculated baby step?
Is it keeping your feet right where they are but lifting up your chin to look at Him?
Is it simply turning yourself around so your face is toward Him instead of your back?

Be honest about where you are now and what next move your heart is ready for. You'll see as you go along here how God really does have great love for you and how He already made the first move. You'll see how He's waiting with more patience than you'll ever understand for you to make *your* next move.

But He understands it's a process. He'll gladly receive whatever you'll give Him, as long as it's honest. He knows there are things about Him you don't yet know. He can't wait to meet you wherever you are and show you more.

So much more.

How to Use This Book

First, use this book slowly.

This book is not meant to fill your head with more information *about* God and who He is. Rather, it's meant to help you connect your heart with God's heart in an uncomplicated and unhurried way. Connections like this, and the revelations that await you, are what will truly transform you, your life, and your faith.

Go at the pace your heart is ready for. There are forty days included, but don't feel you have to rush through and be finished in exactly forty days. This isn't that type of book. One day can take a whole week if you want it to. Push yourself a little to keep moving forward, but don't pressure yourself to get it done by a fixed deadline.

Secondly, use this book like a steady guide or trusted map.

Let this book be a tool in your hands accompanying you along your way. It's a tool that's meant to feel manageable, doable. It's not meant to feel intimidating or mentally exhausting. Short, simple sentences and white space on the page were intentional. Any repetition is meant to feel like an echo, not a redundancy.

You'll notice how each day begins and ends with the same scripture. This was intentional too. Read the verse each time. Don't skip past it. Remind yourself to slow down and read *each* verse *each time*.

Take note of what rises up to the surface in your heart, and carry those things with you in your mind and in your focus as you go about your day.

Go on and get to know the One who loves you more than you'll ever comprehend. Let Him show you things about Himself you have not yet known.

Lean in; don't pull away. Give your heart time to engage.

Don't rush through. Settle in, and take it slow.

Remember, it's not meant to be complicated. Give yourself breathing room.

Enjoy the process.

Now, take a deep breath, settle in for a few minutes, and when you're ready, turn the page.

Breathe

Day 1

*In his hand is the life of every living thing
and the breath of all mankind.*
—Job 12:10 (ESV)

Take a deep breath in. Hold it for a second. Now slowly let it out.

Let your mind wander.

Let your mind wander over your recent days.

What's been on your schedule? What's been on your mind? What's been on your *heart*?

What's been enjoyable? What's been hard?

Now think about God for a moment. Don't rush. Settle in.

What comes to mind when you think about Him?

Is there anywhere in your recent days where you can *honestly* say you saw evidence of God—anything that might reveal His heart, His character, or even His very existence? (It's OK to let yourself be honest here.)

Have you ever stopped to really consider that idea?

Seeing evidence of where God is at work in our lives doesn't always come easily.

You have to sort of train your eyes a bit. Give them time to adjust.

If you're not sure where to start, consider this:

When you opened your eyes this morning and took your first waking breath, *there*.

There He was. Right there, in that very moment. And He was with you all day, a steady and rhythmic reminder of His presence in every inhale and every exhale.

Breathe in. Breathe out. Breathe in. Breathe out.

The very presence of the Father is *that close*. Keep this truth in mind as you go about your day today. And no matter what comes your way later, don't forget to breathe.

Big breath in ... and hold ... and big breath out.

It's no more complicated than that.

> *In his hand is the life of every living thing*
> *and the breath of all mankind.*
> —Job 12:10 (ESV)

Day 2

In his hand is the life of every living thing
and the breath of all mankind.
—Job 12:10 (ESV)

Today, just breathe.

Breathe in ... breathe out ... breathe in ... breathe out.

Breathe in God's strength. Breathe out your anxiety. (Psalm. 55:22)*

Breathe in His peace. Breathe out your confusion. (1 Corinthians 14:33)

Breathe in His stillness. Breathe out your restlessness. (Psalm 46:10)

Breathe in His acceptance. Breathe out rejection. (John 6:37)

Breathe in His grace. Breathe out condemnation. (Romans 8:1)

Breathe in His rest. Breathe out your weariness. (Matthew 11:28)

Breathe in His love. Breathe out your fear. (1 John 4:18)

Read this verse slowly:

> Whenever my busy thoughts were out of control, the soothing comfort of your presence calmed me down and overwhelmed me with delight. (Psalm 94:19 TPT)

Let these truths settle you, as they settle deep into that part of your soul where you need Him the most today.

Big breath in ... and hold ... and big breath out.

It's no more complicated than that.

> *In his hand is the life of every living thing*
> *and the breath of all mankind.*
> —Job 12:10 (ESV)

*You can find these scripture verses at the end of this book in the Scripture References section.

Day 3

In his hand is the life of every living thing
and the breath of all mankind.
—Job 12:10 (ESV)

Which breath did you need to take the most yesterday?

(Go back and review the list if you need to.)

Was it a breath of God's strength, truth, or stillness? Was it a breath of His acceptance, grace, rest, or love? Perhaps something else came to mind.

Take a few deep breaths while you focus on just that one thing.

Don't rush. Take your time with this.

Read this verse slowly:

> Whenever my busy thoughts were out of control,
> the soothing comfort of your presence calmed me
> down and overwhelmed me with delight. (Psalm
> 94:19 TPT)

Now go ahead and read it again, out loud. If it feels awkward, that's all right. Embrace it. You need to hear yourself say it, even if it's just a whisper. Reciting scripture out loud, in your own voice, is more powerful than you know. Go ahead.

Carry this one with you today:

When you feel the grip of anxiety, fear, or whatever it is trying to take hold of you, stop. Take a moment, and take a breath. Let your mind and heart return here, to this space, and read Psalm 94:19.

Make this sentence personal:

Breathe in God's _____; breathe out _____.

It's no more complicated than that.

> *In his hand is the life of every living thing*
> *and the breath of all mankind.*
> —Job 12:10 (ESV)

Day 4

In his hand is the life of every living thing
and the breath of all mankind.
—Job 12:10 (ESV)

Today is a new day, and His mercies are new every morning.
(Lamentations 3:22–23)

Breathe *that* one in!

Every day is the start of something new.

Today offers you a new opportunity for exploration and discovery
into the heart of God—who He is and where He is at work in your
life.

Everything is new today.

Look for Him. Take note of the moments where you see Him.

Start training your eyes to see where He is, instead of where you perceive
He isn't.

Yes, He is indeed in every breath you take, and there's so much more for you to see.

It may take some time for your eyes to adjust, but as they do, the awe and wonder of it all will change everything.

God is bigger than you know; He's closer than you realize; and He's so much better than you thought He was. Let Him show you.

Take a big breath in … and hold … and let it out.

It's not complicated.

He's right there.

He's with you right now, today, and He'll be there again in the morning when you wake up.

> *In his hand is the life of every living thing*
> *and the breath of all mankind.*
> —Job 12:10 (ESV)

Day 5

*In his hand is the life of every living thing
and the breath of all mankind.*
—Job 12:10 (ESV)

Think about the first three words of Job 12:10: *in his hand.*

Now take a deep breath and think about God's hand for a moment.

What comes to mind?

Is His hand open or closed?

Is His hand outstretched, or is His finger pointing at you?

Is His hand motioning you closer or pushing you away?

Give yourself permission to really think about this.

Don't rush. This part matters.

Since your very life is in God's hand, your honest view of Him and His hand matters.

Take a couple of days to only focus on this if you need to. It's that important.

But know this: God longs for you to clearly see the truth of who He is. And He knows it's a process and that it takes time. He's not in a rush, so you needn't be either. He'll go at your pace. He'll match you step for step.

No matter where we are, none of us see the complete picture of who God is. We're all on a path of discovery.

A simple place to start is with the following prayer:

God, I don't know you well enough. Help me to see the truth of who You are.

Take a breath, and let your own journey of discovery begin.

In his hand is the life of every living thing
and the breath of all mankind.
—Job 12:10 (ESV)

Day 6

*In his hand is the life of every living thing
and the breath of all mankind.*
—Job 12:10 (ESV)

In His hand is the life of every living thing.

That means your life *too.*

That means He's holding onto you *too.*

On days when you can feel it and days when you can't,

He's there holding onto you.

On days when you're holding tightly onto Him,

He's there holding onto you.

On days when you don't feel like holding onto Him at all,

He's there holding onto you.

On days when it's obvious and days when it doesn't seem true,

He's there holding onto you.

Strong and unwavering, He's never changing His mind about you.

He held onto you all day yesterday, and He'll hold onto you all day again today.

Take a deep breath of that truth in.

Take a deep breath in, let it out, and let yourself be held.

He's that close. Steady and constant.

Truth.

In his hand is the life of every living thing
and the breath of all mankind.
—Job 12:10 (ESV)

Day 7

In his hand is the life of every living thing
and the breath of all mankind.
—Job 12:10 (ESV)

Let your mind wander for a moment as you think over your week.

Now let your mind wander for a moment as you think about *God*.

Take a big breath in … and hold … and let it out.

Again—big breath in … and hold … and let it out.

Take a minute to thank God for that breath in your lungs.

Thank Him for His steady presence that is *always* with you.

Thank Him for His steady hand that is *always* holding you.

Consider Psalm 94:19 again today:

> Whenever my busy thoughts were out of control,
> the soothing comfort of your presence calmed me
> down and overwhelmed me with delight. (TPT)

The gap between busy, out-of-control thoughts and the calm that comes with His presence isn't always a quick one to bridge. Don't get discouraged.

Start training your eyes to begin seeing where He *is*, instead of where you perceive He *isn't* or must not be.

It may take a little practice, so give it time. Let your eyes adjust.

Focus on your breath. Now focus on Him. Know that He's right *there*.

It's no more complicated than that.

In his hand is the life of every living thing
and the breath of all mankind.
—Job 12:10 (ESV)

Near

Day 8

His purpose was for the nations to seek after God and perhaps feel their way toward him and find him— though he is not far from any one of us.
—Acts 17:27 (NLT)

When you think about God, does He feel near or far these days?

Take a minute to really think about that.

It's a normal part of the process to have days when He feels so close and other days when He feels so far away.

Whatever you're feeling, be honest about it. The only right answer here is an honest answer.

If He feels close, thank Him and rest in His tangible presence today. Linger with Him.

If He feels far, talk to Him about it. It can be as simple as this:

God, you feel far right now. Please show me where you are.

And then just breathe—no stressing or striving. Just give yourself a moment to breathe.

Take a big breath in … and let it out … and breathe in again … and let it out.

He's right there. He's always right there.

It's no more complicated than that.

Give it time. Your eyes will adjust. You have permission to be right where you are.

God will help you see what you couldn't see before.

> *His purpose was for the nations to seek after God and*
> *perhaps feel their way toward him and find him—*
> *though he is not far from any one of us.*
> —Acts 17:27 (NLT)

(Remember, take the time to read each verse *each time*. Don't skip over the verse at the end. Repetition like this is intentional and important.)

Day 9

*His purpose was for the nations to seek after God and
perhaps feel their way toward him and find him—
though he is not far from any one of us.*
—Acts 17:27 (NLT)

Think about the last part of Acts 17:27: "though he is *not far* from
any one of us" (emphasis added).

That is profound and that is the truth.

He is not far.

A truth like that will anchor your soul on days when life is knocking
you around a bit.

A truth like that helps bridge the gap between busy, out-of-control
thoughts and experiencing the soothing comfort of his presence that
will calm you down.

Take a second to read Psalm 94:19 again.

Whenever my busy thoughts were out of control,
the soothing comfort of your presence calmed me
down and overwhelmed me with delight. (TPT)

Your feelings are real, they are valid, and they are important.

But feelings don't always reflect the truth about a situation.

On days when God *feels* far away, don't let your feelings sweep you out to sea.

Take a moment to breathe, and remember you do have an anchor.

You have this truth:

God is *not far* from any one of us.

Not far. Near. Truth.

> *His purpose was for the nations to seek after God and*
> *perhaps feel their way toward him and find him—*
> *though he is not far from any one of us.*
> —Acts 17:27 (NLT)

Day 10

His purpose was for the nations to seek after God and
perhaps feel their way toward him and find him—
though he is not far from any one of us.
—Acts 17:27 (NLT)

Think about this profound phrase tucked into Acts 17:27: "feel their way toward him."

You know what that means?

It means faith is a process. You don't have to arrive all at once.

It means God is a patient God, and He's patient with your process.

It means you have breathing room.

It means you're allowed to have questions. You're allowed to not be sure about everything right away.

Just because you've pointed your steps in His direction, that doesn't mean you'll never have any questions—or doubts—along the way.

So go ahead. Take a deep breath, and be honest with yourself about the questions and doubts you have.

Then be honest with God about those very things. He wants to hear from you in your own voice about what's really going on in your heart.

He wants to help you as you feel your way toward Him.

Take a deep breath, and know faith is a process.

Just breathe.

It's a process—a beautiful process.

> *His purpose was for the nations to seek after God and*
> *perhaps feel their way toward him and find him—*
> *though he is not far from any one of us.*
> —Acts 17:27 (NLT)

Day 11

*His purpose was for the nations to seek after God and
perhaps feel their way toward him and find him—
though he is not far from any one of us.*
—Acts 17:27 (NLT)

Some days God just feels so *hidden*, doesn't He?

Despite your best efforts to cling to the truth and remind yourself
that He is not far, some days are just tough.

It can feel like God is hiding from you—or worse—that He's hiding
from you *on purpose.*

Know that God is not hiding from you, on purpose or otherwise.

He may feel hidden, but He is certainly not hiding.

Think of stargazing into the night sky. It doesn't always look
impressive right away. But the longer you gaze, the more your eyes
adjust, and the more stars you see.

The same stars were always there, though they may have appeared hidden at first. But they weren't really hiding. Your eyes just needed some time to adjust.

Seeing evidence of where God is in your life is just like that. At first He may appear to be hidden. But then your eyes adjust, and you start to see what you couldn't before.

And then the awe and wonder sets in, and suddenly you're having a completely different experience.

It's a process. Give it time.

Take a deep breath, look up, and simply gaze.

He's closer than you think.

It's no more complicated than that.

> *"His purpose was for the nations to seek after God*
> *and perhaps feel their way toward him and find*
> *him—though he is not far from any one of us.*
> —Acts 17:27 (NLT)

Day 12

His purpose was for the nations to seek after God and
perhaps feel their way toward him and find him—
though he is not far from any one of us.
—Acts 17:27 (NLT)

Think about these three words you just read in Acts 17:27: "and find him."

God is *findable*. That means He is able to be found!

In fact, you would never be able to find Him if He hadn't made Himself findable.

And if His purpose was that we would find Him, that means He *wants* to be found!

God is not playing a game of hide-and-seek where He's the one hiding and doesn't want to be found by you, the one seeking.

It's not like that at all. In fact, He's purposely giving away His position all the time so you can easily find Him first!

Sit still for a minute. All you need to do is breathe ... and listen.

When it's quiet enough, just listen to your own breathing for a moment.

That sound you hear?

That's Him. He's right there. You just found Him.

You just found Him in an odd little hiding place, right there under your very nose.

On days when God feels hidden, you can always return here to this simple truth that He really is that close and that obvious.

He's not hiding or trying to tease you. He's not playing hard to get. He very much wants to be got!

Breathe. Just breathe.

> *His purpose was for the nations to seek after God and*
> *perhaps feel their way toward him and find him—*
> *though he is not far from any one of us.*
> —Acts 17:27 (NLT)

Day 13

*His purpose was for the nations to seek after God and
perhaps feel their way toward him and find him—
though he is not far from any one of us.*
—Acts 17:27 (NLT)

So if God is not hiding and He wants you to find Him, perhaps it's
more like God is … *waiting*?

God gives us this promise in Jeremiah 29:13:

> If you look for me wholeheartedly, you will find me. (NLT)

He's waiting for you to look for Him.

He's there, patiently waiting for your gaze to meet His.

He's waiting for your eyes to adjust and see Him for who He truly
is and where He is working in your life.

Looking for Him wholeheartedly means looking *away* from things
that distract your heart.

Anxiety, confusion, restlessness, condemnation, weariness, and fear can all serve as those distractions.

Take a moment to think back to days 2 and 3. Which breath did you need to take the most? That might be a hint as to what may be distracting your heart and preventing you from seeing God clearly.

Breathe it out, and breathe Him in.

It's a process. Don't rush it. Give it time.

Steady your gaze and breathe.

Just breathe.

> *His purpose was for the nations to seek after God and*
> *perhaps feel their way toward him and find him—*
> *though he is not far from any one of us.*
> —Acts 17:27 (NLT)

Day 14

*His purpose was for the nations to seek after God and
perhaps feel their way toward him and find him—
though he is not far from any one of us.*
—Acts 17:27 (NLT)

Take a big breath in … and hold … and slowly let it out.

Go ahead and let your mind wander as you think over your week.

Reflect for a minute about how near or far God has felt to you.

Remind yourself that it's OK to be exactly where you are.

Remind yourself that training your eyes to see where He is at work
in your life takes time. Your eyes will adjust. It's a process.

However, on days when God feels far and you feel like you're losing
your footing, take a deep breath, steady yourself, and remind yourself
of these two truths:

- God is not far (though some days he may *feel* far).
- God is not hiding from you (though some days he may *feel*
  hidden).

Breathe out those things that are distracting your heart, and breathe in the truth of who He is.

Steady your gaze once again on Him, and just breathe.

And consider that perhaps what we too quickly perceive as Him hiding is actually Him *waiting*—waiting for you to call out to Him.

> *His purpose was for the nations to seek after God and*
> *perhaps feel their way toward him and find him—*
> *though he is not far from any one of us.*
> —Acts 17:27 (NLT)

Call

Day 15

Call to me and I will answer you,
and will tell you great and hidden things that you have not known.
—Jeremiah 33:3 (ESV)

God is approachable.

You can go to Him. You can call out to Him—exactly as you are right now.

Your good behavior on your good days doesn't make Him any *more* approachable.

Your bad behavior on your bad days doesn't make Him any *less* approachable.

He's just there—always there, ready and waiting.

Open arms—strong and steady.

Just breathe.

He's waiting, not hiding.

Turn your face toward Him. Meet His gaze. Lock eyes.

See that He's not cold, unconcerned, or distant.

See that He's warm, gentle, attentive, and ... *near.*

He's approachable and available.

All day long. All night long.

Available. Always.

You can go to Him and call out to Him, now and all throughout your day.

Call to me and I will answer you,
and will tell you great and hidden things that you have not known.
—Jeremiah 33:3 (ESV)

Day 16

Call to me and I will answer you,
and will tell you great and hidden things that you have not known.
—Jeremiah 33:3 (ESV)

Think about the first three words of Jeremiah 33:3 today: "call to me."

It's an invitation. Do you hear it?

Take a deep breath, and just listen for a minute. The God of the universe is inviting you into something so much deeper than you know. He's inviting you into a deeper connection with *Him*.

He wants to hear from you. You're *allowed* to call out to Him.

He's inviting you.

So call out to Him with whatever is on your mind and with whatever is on your heart.

Call out to Him with your questions. Call out to Him with your concerns.

Call out to Him with a loud voice. Call out to Him in a quiet whisper.

Just call out to Him.

Not out of a place of arrogance demanding He answer you. No, call out to Him with a humble heart acknowledging that you need Him.

Take a deep breath, turn your focus back to Him, and steady your gaze there.

It's an act of humility and surrender and perfectly positions you to receive revelation from Him.

Take your time. When you're ready, call out to Him. But remember to do so *humbly*.

He's right there.

Waiting, not hiding.

Call to me and I will answer you,
and will tell you great and hidden things that you have not known.
—Jeremiah 33:3 (ESV)

Day 17

Call to me and I will answer you,
and will tell you great and hidden things that you have not known.
—Jeremiah 33:3 (ESV)

Today just think about this next part of Jeremiah 33:3: "and I will answer you."

First He offers you an invitation. Then He gives you a promise.

God promises to answer you. It's a promise to answer your call, though perhaps not your every question.

That doesn't mean you shouldn't bring Him your questions. He wants to hear from you!

It means your *call* won't go unanswered. It means He won't ignore you or push you away.

He may not answer your question, but not because He doesn't care or considers it insignificant. Sometimes He cares more about why you're asking the question in the first place—what's just below the surface driving it.

He may reveal things to you there in *that place* that will leave you face down in awe and wonder of who He is and how well He knows you.

Since you know He's going to answer your call, be intentional about listening for Him and seeing Him. Train your ears and eyes to notice where you see Him and how He's answering you, where He's answering you.

Don't forget to breathe. Slow down. Patience.

Take a big breath in … and let it out.

Steady.

Breathe out distractions one by one, and breathe Him in.

Let Him answer you. You've called out to Him; now let Him answer you.

Call to me and I will answer you,
and will tell you great and hidden things that you have not known.
—Jeremiah 33:3 (ESV)

Day 18

Call to me and I will answer you,
and will tell you great and hidden things that you have not known.
—Jeremiah 33:3 (ESV)

Today just think about these words from Jeremiah 33:3: "and will tell you."

You've called out to Him and are waiting for Him to answer you.

What to do while you wait?

Breathe. Just breathe.

Breathe out your impatience. Breathe in His presence.

Breathe out your restlessness. Breathe in His peace.

Breathe out your doubt. Breathe in His truth.

He has promised to answer your call. God *wants* to talk to you.

God designed you to hear Him. He wouldn't try talking to you if He hadn't.

Just because you may not hear Him, that doesn't mean He's not answering you.

Often it's a matter of training your ears to hear Him and your eyes to see Him.

This part is a process, and it takes time.

Steady. Patience. Breathe.

You were made to hear Him. You were made to see Him. Give it time.

He wants you to hear Him. He wants you to see Him.

Call to me and I will answer you,
and will tell you great and hidden things that you have not known.
—Jeremiah 33:3 (ESV)

Day 19

Call to me and I will answer you,
and will tell you great and hidden things that you have not known.
—Jeremiah 33:3 (ESV)

Consider these curious little words in the middle of Jeremiah 33:3 today: "great and hidden things."

Other translations have put it in these ways:

- *great and mighty things* (NASB)
- *great and unsearchable things* (NIV)

God indeed has so much He wants to share with you, but what does He mean by *great and hidden things*?

Sometimes it means He has great and hidden things to explain to you about your past—things that haven't made sense or things you've misunderstood along the way.

Other times He may have great and mighty things to tell you about your future—what's up ahead and where you're going.

But perhaps the *best part* is that it means He has great and unsearchable things about *Himself* He's longing to reveal to you that only He can.

He cares so very much that you are seeing Him clearly for the truth of who He is. He longs to show you *truth*.

However, sometimes the truth He reveals can be a little hard to hear.

Lean in anyway. Trust Him through it.

Know that condemnation and guilt are never His intention or His goal.

His heart for you is only that of love—a love like you've never known.

So listen for Him. Look for Him. He's not far. He's not hiding. You can trust Him.

Call out to Him for He promises to answer you. Let Him.

Call to me and I will answer you,
and will tell you great and hidden things that you have not known.
—Jeremiah 33:3 (ESV)

Day 20

Call to me and I will answer you,
and will tell you great and hidden things that you have not known.
—Jeremiah 33:3 (ESV)

Today just focus on the last part of Jeremiah 33:3: "you have not known."

Take a deep breath, and settle in for this truth:

God knows there are things that you don't yet know.

There is grace and plentiful breathing room for all the things you don't yet know.

You have questions about your life. You have questions about yourself.

You have small questions, and you have big questions.

You have questions about so many things. You even have questions about *Him*.

God welcomes your questions, and better yet, encourages them.

He doesn't expect you to know everything all the time. Breathe that in.

He doesn't expect you to know everything all the time.

He knows your faith is a process. He knows things take time.

Hearing Him takes time. Seeing Him takes time. Getting to know Him takes time.

Breathe. Just breathe.

He knows there are things you don't yet know.

Call out to Him. Listen for Him.

Let Him answer you and tell you of great and hidden things you have not known.

Call to me and I will answer you,
and will tell you great and hidden things that you have not known.
—Jeremiah 33:3 (ESV)

Day 21

Call to me and I will answer you,
and will tell you great and hidden things that you have not known.
—Jeremiah 33:3 (ESV)

Call to me

God is approachable. You can go to Him. He's waiting, not hiding. He's inviting you to approach Him, and come to Him. Do so with humility.

And I will answer you

God promises to answer your call, though He may not always answer your questions.

You've called to Him. Now listen for Him. Look for Him. Be patient. Let Him answer you.

And will tell you

He has promised to answer your call. He wants to talk to you! You were designed to hear Him. You were designed to see Him.

Great and hidden things
God longs to show you great and hidden things that are anchored in *truth*.

These great and hidden things are about you, your life, and—most importantly—about *Him*.

You have not known
God knows there are things you don't yet know.
Call out to Him. Listen for Him. Let Him answer you and tell you of great and hidden things you have not known.

Call to me and I will answer you,
and will tell you great and hidden things that you have not known.
—Jeremiah 33:3 (ESV)

Focus

Day 22

You will keep in perfect peace all who trust in you,
all whose thoughts are fixed on you!
—Isaiah 26:3 (NLT)

Peace, perfect peace—can you even imagine? It hardly seems possible.

And yet that's what God is offering to those who will truly seek to trust Him and fix their thoughts on Him.

He's offering an alternative to the confusion, anxiety, worry, and stress that you are confronted with and held down by in your life.

In this beautiful promise He's telling you there is *another way*.

A better way. A higher way.

Look up.

There *is* another way through.

The way is simple but not always easy.

Instead of focusing on the problems in front of you, He's inviting you to focus on Him instead—to see Him for where He *is* and not for where you perceive He *isn't*.

It takes practice. It takes time. It takes perseverance. It's a process.

But yes, there *is* another way available to you.

And peace, overwhelming peace, peace that hardly makes sense (Philippians 4:7) is what He's offering to those who would but dare choose to trust Him and steady their gaze on Him alone.

Take a deep breath and read this verse slowly:

> For God is not a God of confusion, but of
> peace. (1 Corinthians 14:33 ESV)

> *You will keep in perfect peace all who trust in you,*
> *all whose thoughts are fixed on you!*
> —Isaiah 26:3 (NLT)

Day 23

You will keep in perfect peace all who trust in you,
all whose thoughts are fixed on you!
—Isaiah 26:3 (NLT)

How do you practically look at Jesus and fix your thoughts on Him?
What does that look like?

Is this something that comes naturally to you? If it's not, try starting
with a focal point.

Here are some things you could focus on to help get you started:

- *a Bible verse* that connects with your heart that you commit
  to memory
- *a worship song* that gets stuck in your head all day you can't
  help but sing
- *an attribute* like God's peace, strength, love, or forgiveness
- *an image* like the cross or an open Bible
- *something from nature* like a sunset, water, trees, or a butterfly

Whatever you choose, let it be something that connects you to the
truth of who Jesus is—something symbolic of His heart, His nature,

and His character. (Experiment and have fun with this! Try a couple different ones this week until you find one that's easy for you to connect with and feels most natural.)

A focal point will serve as a place in your mind for all those busy thoughts and swirling emotions to land—a place where your mind can go to simply stop for a minute, find some breathing room, and regroup.

But it's not just that. It will become a practical place where your heart and mind can go to connect with Jesus, no matter where you are or what you are doing.

It will become your mental cue to look up, focus on Jesus, and anchor your thoughts there—on Him.

He is your anchor. He is your constant.

He is your ever-present help in times of trouble (Psalm 46:1).

A focal point will help you as you train your heart to focus on and worship Him instead of your problems.

You will keep in perfect peace all who trust in you,
all whose thoughts are fixed on you!
—Isaiah 26:3 (NLT)

Day 24

You will keep in perfect peace all who trust in you,
all whose thoughts are fixed on you!
—Isaiah 26:3 (NLT)

Start today by asking yourself this honest question: *What takes your focus throughout the day?*

What takes your *real* focus, your *deep* focus—the deep focus of your heart?

Where does your mind naturally drift in mundane moments?

Do things like worry, anxiety, anger, fear, or bitterness steal the focus of your heart?

It doesn't have to be this way. There is another way—a higher way.

Find your focal point. (Flip back to day 23 for a few suggestions if you need help.)

Now focus.

Breathe. Just breathe.

In moments like this know that He's near, not far.

Steady.

Focus on Him until He becomes bigger than the problem in front of you.

Train your eyes to look around and see where He *is* instead of where you perceive He *isn't*.

When your focus drifts and wanders, bring it back. Take a deep breath and find your focal point once more.

Let His steady presence calm you down and overwhelm you with delight.

Read this, and breathe deeply:

Whenever my busy thoughts were out of control, the soothing comfort of your presence calmed me down and overwhelmed me with delight. Psalm 94:19 (TPT)

> *You will keep in perfect peace all who trust in you,*
> *all whose thoughts are fixed on you!*
> —Isaiah 26:3 (NLT)

Day 25

You will keep in perfect peace all who trust in you,
all whose thoughts are fixed on you!
—Isaiah 26:3 (NLT)

Take a deep breath.

Find your focal point from day 23. Picture it. Stare at it.

Settle in.

It's just you … and *Him* now.

Let everything else fall away.

It's just you … and *Jesus* … now in this sacred moment.

Focus. Don't wander. Focus.

You've drawn near; now watch His next move. His face is beaming. His arms are open. See His footsteps? They're steady and rhythmic. He's closing the gap.

You've called out to Him; now listen as He answers you.

Listen as He tells you to look at Him, just look at Him.

Peace—overwhelming peace is found here in His presence.

Tell your busy heart to stop for a minute and just ... rest.

Rest in His gaze; rest in His love.

Rest in this moment.

And breathe. Just breathe.

You will keep in perfect peace all who trust in you,
all whose thoughts are fixed on you!
—Isaiah 26:3 (NLT)

Day 26

You will keep in perfect peace all who trust in you,
all whose thoughts are fixed on you!
—Isaiah 26:3 (NLT)

Breathe. Just breathe.

Find your focal point. (Or choose a new one to try out today!)

Steady your gaze there. Steady your thoughts there. Don't wander; bring it back. Focus.

Move out of your own way and allow your heart to simply look at Jesus. Let your heart gaze. Let your heart stare.

See that He's near, not far.

See the love in His eyes, the purity of His heart. See the smile on His face.

He's inviting you in. He's inviting you closer. He wants to show you the truth of who He is.

Breathe. Just breathe.

Take Him in. He's everything you want and everything you need. And He's right there—waiting, not hiding.

Go on; get to know Him.

Allow Him to show you something about Himself you have not yet known.

Don't rush; let your heart linger. He's so much ... *more* ... than you ever thought He was. Stare at Him. For the rest of your days, train your eyes to intently stare at Him.

Let Him show you the truth of who He is.

Truth that will change everything.

> *You will keep in perfect peace all who trust in you,*
> *all whose thoughts are fixed on you!*
> —Isaiah 26:3 (NLT)

Day 27

You will keep in perfect peace all who trust in you,
all whose thoughts are fixed on you!
—Isaiah 26:3 (NLT)

Take a deep breath, and remind yourself that it's a process.

Getting to know God is a process. Focusing on Him is a process. Trusting Him is a process.

Start with where you are. There's no pressure to be anywhere else.

Breathe. Just breathe.

You don't have to wait until you've arrived to experience His peace.

It's available to you right now right where you are.

Because God knows there are things you don't yet know. He knows it's a process.

Start with where you are. Start by glancing at Him if staring feels awkward.

The more you catch a glimpse of Him, the more you'll want to see. The more you want to see, the more you'll find yourself staring.

But don't rush. Give your heart time.

Tell God you don't know Him well enough, and ask Him to show you something about Himself that you don't yet know.

Start there, and don't forget to breathe.

Know that there's grace and beautiful breathing room for your heart to settle down and take in what He longs to show you.

> *You will keep in perfect peace all who trust in you,*
> *all whose thoughts are fixed on you!*
> —Isaiah 26:3 (NLT)

Day 28

You will keep in perfect peace all who trust in you,
all whose thoughts are fixed on you!
—Isaiah 26:3 (NLT)

Today, just breathe.

Find your focal point. (Hopefully there's one that is starting to feel easy and natural for you. If not, don't get discouraged. This, too, may take a little time. Don't rush it. Call out to the Lord, and ask Him to help show you a focal point that will be a unique connecting point between you and Him.)

Now focus.

Breathe in, and breathe out. Breathe in, and breathe out.

Focus on Him.

Listen as He invites you to come up higher.

Go with Him.

Let Him show you things about Himself you don't yet know.

Fix your thoughts on Him. Fix the gaze of your heart on Him.

When you wander, come on back. It's a process.

But know that He's waiting, not hiding—always waiting, never hiding.

Embrace the silence. Embrace the stillness.

Peace, perfect peace, overwhelming peace is here in this moment as your heart locks eyes with Jesus, and you can't help but stare.

Don't rush. Stay a little longer. Linger here with Him.

And breathe. Just breathe.

You will keep in perfect peace all who trust in you,
all whose thoughts are fixed on you!
—Isaiah 26:3 (NLT)

Move

Day 29

Move your heart closer and closer to God,
and he will come even closer to you.
—James 4:8 (TPT)

Take a deep breath in … and slowly let it out.

Find your focal point (see day 23).

Settle in.

What's busy on your mind, busy on your heart?

Does God *feel* near or far?

When you think about moving your heart closer to God, what does that next move look like?

It's OK to start with where you are.

Breathe out those familiar things that are distracting your heart.

Breathe out doubt, worry, confusion, fear, anxiety, and condemnation.

Now breathe in His truth. Breathe in His presence.

Remind your heart of what is true.

Don't pull away; lean in.

Look up, and look at Him. Stare at Him.

Call out to Him.

Prepare your heart to move closer to Him.

> *Move your heart closer and closer to God,*
> *and he will come even closer to you.*
> —James 4:8 (TPT)

Day 30

Move your heart closer and closer to God,
and he will come even closer to you.
—James 4:8 (TPT)

Read the following verse that's repeated from the "Near" chapter.

"His purpose was for the nations to seek after God and perhaps feel their way toward him and find him—though he is not far from any one of us" (Acts 17:27 NLT).

God is not out there in the distance somewhere waiting for you to make the first move to begin closing the gap.

He's near, not far.

He's already made the first move to show how much He loves us.

Take a deep breath, and read this verse slowly:

But God showed His great love for us by sending Christ to die for us while we were still sinners. (Romans 5:8 NLT)

Take a deep breath, and think about that one for a moment.

God has great love for us—for *you*—so much so that He already made the first move.

And it was a big move.

It was an extravagant move demonstrating His extravagant love.

God loves us with *that* kind of love before we even love Him back.

Don't rush through this part. Settle in for a minute. Just look up, and look at Him.

Know that He loves you more than you'll ever comprehend.

Breathe that love deep into your heart today.

Move your heart closer and closer to God,
and he will come even closer to you.
—James 4:8 (TPT)

Day 31

Move your heart closer and closer to God,
and he will come even closer to you.
—James 4:8 (TPT)

God wants to talk to you.

He wants to be close to you.

Call out to Him. Move your heart a little closer to Him.

No effort you make is wasted or goes unnoticed by Him.

No whisper, glance, or baby step is too small that He would say it somehow wasn't enough.

Your heart is enough.

He loves you a massive amount. Your efforts matter to Him.

It's not complicated. Simply turn your focus to Him.

See that He's closing the gap between you and Him.

See Him walking toward you, His face beaming, eyes full of love.

As you lock your eyes on Him, see how His eyes were already locked on you.

See His footsteps, steady and rhythmic.

He's closing the gap. He's heading your way.

Go to Him.

Make your move.

> *Move your heart closer and closer to God,*
> *and he will come even closer to you.*
> —James 4:8 (TPT)

Day 32

Move your heart closer and closer to God,
and he will come even closer to you.
—James 4:8 (TPT)

Moving your heart closer and closer to God is the journey of a lifetime.

Start with where you are, and move on from there.

The closer you get, the closer you'll want to be.

There will always be more of Him to see, more of Him to discover.

More depth. More revelation. More truth.

So go on, get to know Him a little more day-by-day.

Enjoy the process. Enjoy the discovery.

A simple place for you to start:

"God, I don't know you well enough. Show me something about You I don't yet know."

Take a deep breath, and listen. Listen now, and listen throughout your day.

He's waiting, not hiding. He's near, not far. Don't rush things.

Set your mind to move your heart a little closer every day.

Leap by leap. Step by step. Glance by glance.

Discover how He's so much better than you ever thought He was.

Move your heart closer and closer to God,
and he will come even closer to you.
—James 4:8 (TPT)

Day 33

Move your heart closer and closer to God,
and he will come even closer to you.
—James 4:8 (TPT)

As you are discovering what it looks like for you to move your heart closer and closer to Jesus, there's one step you absolutely must take—one move you absolutely must make.

If you have not already done so, you must take the step of surrendering your life to Jesus Christ and asking Him to be your Lord and Savior.

It's a big step, but it's a beautiful one. Don't rush through this part.

This isn't the kind of step you take lightly or do out of pressure, guilt, or obligation.

It's a step you take as the response of your heart when you consider all Jesus has already done for you.

Read John 3:16–17 slowly:

For God so loved the world, that He gave His only Son, that whoever believes in Him should not perish but have eternal life. For God did not send His Son into the world to condemn the world, but in order that the world might be saved through Him. (ESV)

Think about that for a moment.

Then when you're ready ... take a deep breath, settle in, and pray this prayer:

> *Jesus, thank You for making the first move. Thank You for willingly going to the cross to die for my sins—an extravagant move that made a way for me to come back to You. I repent of my sins and ask for Your forgiveness. Fill me with Your Holy Spirit, the Helper, to help me live a new life that is pleasing to You. Help me work through the questions and doubts I still have, and help me see the truth of who You are a little more each and every day. Amen.*

It's no more complicated than that.

After you take this step, let your next step be a step (or leap!) of great celebration and freedom. You've been forgiven! Everything is new now! Your sins of yesterday are behind you! You now have full assurance that when you die, you will go to heaven where your journey of getting to know Jesus and getting to know the Father will continue throughout all eternity.

Celebrate as you read the following verse:

Yet look at you now! Everything is new! Although you were once distant and far away from God, now you have been brought delightfully close to him through the sacred blood of Jesus–you have actually been united to Christ! (Ephesians 2:13 TPT).

Welcome to the family!

Your adventure of moving your heart closer and closer to God is only getting started.

> *Move your heart closer and closer to God,*
> *and he will come even closer to you.*
> —James 4:8 (TPT)

Day 34

Move your heart closer and closer to God,
and he will come even closer to you.
—James 4:8 (TPT)

Take a deep breath, and think about where you are and where you picture God being.

If the next move you imagine is large, bounding leaps toward Him, do so with abandon.

If that's not what your heart is ready for, think about what's hindering you.

What's keeping you from running toward Him with reckless abandon? What's keeping you from loving God with all your heart, soul, strength, and mind (Luke 10:27)?

Don't rush. Settle in. This part matters.

Are there hurdles and walls that just seem impossible to scale?

Are there past traumas, disappointments, pain, and grief?

Are there old habits you just can't break or sins you keep returning to?

Call out to Him, and humbly ask Him to meet you *there* in *that* place.

Ask Him to help you work through your pain and heal those wounds that cut deep into your heart, to help you confess your sin and repent and accept His forgiveness.

There is no hurdle or hindrance too great that cannot be removed or that could ever separate you from the love He has for you.

Take a deep breath and slowly read the following verse.

> And I am convinced that nothing can ever separate us from God's love. Neither death nor life, neither angels nor demons, neither our fears for today nor our worries about tomorrow—not even the powers of hell can separate us from God's love. No power in the sky above or in the earth below—indeed, nothing in all creation will ever be able to separate us from the love of God that is revealed in Christ Jesus our Lord. (Romans 8:38–39 NLT)

> *Move your heart closer and closer to God,*
> *and he will come even closer to you.*
> —James 4:8 (TPT)

Day 35

Move your heart closer and closer to God,
and he will come even closer to you.
—James 4:8 (TPT)

Take a deep breath, and settle in for a minute. Read James 4:8 *slowly*.

Moving your heart closer and closer to God, this is what you will be doing for the rest of your life.

What a journey, what an adventure awaits you. What stories you will have to tell!

God already made the first move. With gentle patience He's reminding you it's your turn.

Give yourself the permission to start where you are, here on this day.

Leap toward Him, step toward Him, turn toward Him. Lift up your chin, and simply look toward Him.

The closer you get, the closer you'll want to be. Lean in; don't pull away.

Your efforts are enough.

There's nothing standing in your way now that cannot be removed (Romans 8:38–39).

Your heart was made for this. *You* were made for this.

So go on, get to know Him—the *real* Him, the *true* Him.

See how He's so much better than you ever thought He was. And He just keeps getting better and better and better.

See how He loves you more than you'll ever comprehend.

Move your heart closer and closer to God,
And he will come even closer to you.
—James 4:8 (TPT)

Be

Day 36

Be still, and know that I am God.
—Psalm 46:10 (ESV)

Be still for a minute, and just breathe.

Big breath in … and let it out. Big breath in … and let it out.

Slow and steady. Steady and rhythmic.

Read Job 12:10.

"In his hand is the life of every living thing and the breath of all mankind" (ESV).

Remember that when your busy thoughts are spinning out of control (Psalm 94:19), you can always come back here to this space, and just breathe.

Focus on Him, and just breathe.

Breathe in His presence. Breathe in His truth.

See His hand motioning you closer, not pushing you away.

See that He's always near. Always holding you. Always loving you.

See Him for the truth of who He is and not for who you perceive He isn't.

The more you see, the more you'll want to look.

The more you look, the more you'll want to discover.

Be still, and know that He is in every breath you take.

Be still, and read Job 12:10 one more time.

"In his hand is the life of every living thing and the breath of all mankind" (ESV).

Be still and know that He loves you more than you'll ever comprehend.

Be still, and know that I am God.
—Psalm 46:10 (ESV)

Day 37

Be still, and know that I am God.
—Psalm 46:10 (ESV)

Be still for a minute, and just breathe.

Read Acts 17:27.

"His purpose was for the nations to seek after God and perhaps feel their way toward him and find him—though he is not far from any one of us" (NLT).

Let your mind wander, and think about how near or far God *feels* to you now.

If He feels near, linger with Him there. Sit with Him there. Discover more of Him there.

If He feels far, ask Him to show you where He is.

Be still, and listen. Focus on what you now know to be true.

Know that He's near, not far.

Know that He may *appear* hidden, but He's not hiding.

Know that faith is a process. Drawing close to God is a process.

God understands it's a process, and He has more patience for your process than you'll ever know.

Breathe in truth, and breathe out those things that are distracting your heart.

Be still, and read Acts 17:27 one more time.

"His purpose was for the nations to seek after God and perhaps feel their way toward him and find him—though he is not far from any one of us" (NLT).

Be still, and know that He loves you more than you'll ever comprehend.

Be still, and know that I am God.
—Psalm 46:10 (ESV)

Day 38

Be still, and know that I am God.
—Psalm 46:10 (ESV)

Be still for a minute, and just breathe.

Read Jeremiah 33:3.

"Call to me and I will answer you, and will tell you great and hidden things that you have not known" (ESV).

Be still, and let your heart approach God.

Be still, and call out to Him.

Be still, and let Him answer you.

Don't rush. Listen.

And breathe … just breathe.

Breathe out those things that are distracting your heart.

Be still, and let Him tell you great and hidden things you have not known.

Enjoy the process. Enjoy the discovery.

Thank Him for what He reveals to you.

Keep calling out to Him. He has so much more to show you.

Be still, and read Jeremiah 33:3 one more time.

"Call to me and I will answer you, and will tell you great and hidden things that you have not known" (ESV).

Be still, and know that He loves you more than you'll ever comprehend.

Be still, and know that I am God.
—Psalm 46:10 (ESV)

Day 39

Be still, and know that I am God.
—Psalm 46:10 (ESV*)*

Be still for a minute, and just breathe. Breathe out distractions, and breathe Him in.

Read Isaiah 26:3.

"You will keep in perfect peace all who trust in you, all whose thoughts are fixed on you" (NLT).

Remember, God is offering you another way through—a higher way. Look up.

Find your focal point. Settle in. Breathe deep.

Be still, and focus on Jesus. Be still, and let your heart stare at Jesus.

Stare at the One who is able to keep you in perfect peace.

Let your gaze linger.

Take a deep breath, and remember it's a process.

Trusting God is a process.

Give it time.

When your mind wanders, take a breath, and bring it back.

It's no more complicated than that.

Peace. Perfect peace—can you even imagine?

Be still, and read Isaiah 26:3 one more time.

"You will keep in perfect peace all who trust in you, all whose thoughts are fixed on you" (NLT).

Be still, and know He loves you more than you'll ever comprehend.

Be still, and know that I am God.
—Psalm 46:10 (ESV)

Day 40

Be still, and know that I am God.
—Psalm 46:10 (ESV)

Take a deep breath. Settle in.

Read James 4:8.

"Move your heart closer and closer to God and he will come even closer to you" (TPT).

Focus on Jesus. Don't rush. Focus.

Be still, and prepare your heart to move closer to Him.

Consider the extravagant way God demonstrated His extravagant love for you. He sent His only Son to die for you before you ever decided to love Him back.

Breathe deep. What a move He made.

Picture where you are right now and what your next move looks like.

Big or small, any move will move His heart.

Leap toward Him. Step toward Him. Look toward Him. Turn around and simply face Him.

Go back and review day 33 if you need to, and let your next step be the step of asking Jesus to be your Lord and Savior.

Remember, there's nothing in your way that cannot be removed (Romans 8:38–39).

So go ahead.

Make your move.

Be still, and read James 4:8 one more time.

"Move your heart closer and closer to God and he will come even closer to you" (TPT).

Be still, and know that He loves you more than you'll ever comprehend.

Be still, and know that I am God.
—Psalm 46:10 (ESV)

Conclusion

No matter how much you grow or how mature you become in your Christian life, you will never outgrow your need to slow down your pace, take some deep breaths, and refocus your attention back on Jesus. You will never outgrow your need to quiet your soul before Him and breathe deeply of His love and the truth of who He is.

You will never outgrow your need to spend unhurried time with Him.

Your journey of moving your heart closer and closer to the heart of God doesn't end here when you close this book. There will always be more of Him to see, more of Him to experience, and more of Him to *know*.

So much more.

Let Jesus be the One who captures your attention and steals the focus of your heart. Let Him be the One you run to when your soul is empty and longing for so much more than this world has to offer. Everything you're looking for and everything you're longing for is found in Him.

Also, if you took the beautiful step of surrendering your life to Jesus and asking Him to be your Lord and Savior as you read this book, I hope you took time to celebrate!

There are a couple of next steps I would strongly encourage you to take.

First, continue to put into practice the exercises you learned in this book. Make time to open up your Bible and read it every day, even if it's just one verse. If you're not sure where to start, the Gospel of John in the New Testament is a great place. Ask the Holy Spirit to give you wisdom and understanding as you read, and don't be afraid to ask a ton of questions as you go along.

Second, get connected with a local Bible-believing church. The Christian life is not meant to be lived out alone. You need people in your corner to help you, encourage you, and teach you. If you're not sure where to start, call out to the Lord and ask Him to show you where you should go. Community was His idea. He'll show you the way.

And lastly, don't forget to breathe.

Just *breathe*.

Know that He is *near*.

Call out to Him.

Focus on Him.

Move toward Him.

Be with Him.

He loves you more than you know. Let Him show you.

It's no more complicated than that.

Scripture References

Chapter 1

"In his hand is the life of every living thing and the breath of all mankind." (Job 12:10 ESV)

"Cast your cares on the Lord and he will sustain you; he will never let the righteous be shaken." (Psalm 55:22 NIV)

"For God is not a God of confusion but of peace." (1 Corinthians 14:33 ESV)

"Be still, and know that I am God." (Psalm 46:10 ESV)

"And all who come to me, I will embrace and will never turn them away." (John 6:37 TPT)

"So now there is no condemnation for those who belong to Christ Jesus." (Romans 8:1 NLT)

"Come to me, all you who are weary and burdened, and I will give you rest." (Matthew 11:28)

"There is no fear in love, but perfect love casts out fear." (1 John 4:18 ESV)

"Whenever my busy thoughts were out of control, the soothing comfort of your presence calmed me down and overwhelmed me with delight." (Psalm 94:19 TPT)

"The steadfast love of the Lord never ceases; his mercies never come to an end; they are new every morning; great is your faithfulness." (Lamentations 3:22–23 ESV)

Chapter 2
"His purpose was for the nations to seek after God and perhaps feel their way toward him and find him—though he is not far from any one of us." (Acts 17:27 NLT)

"Whenever my busy thoughts were out of control, the soothing comfort of your presence calmed me down and overwhelmed me with delight." (Psalm 94:19 TPT)

"If you look for me wholeheartedly, you will find me." (Jeremiah 29:13 NLT)

Chapter 3
"Call to me and I will answer you, and will tell you great and hidden things that you have not known." (Jeremiah 33:3 ESV)

"Call to Me and I will answer you, and I will tell you great and mighty things, which you do not know." (Jeremiah 33:3 NASB)

"Call to me and I will answer you and tell you great and unsearchable things you do not know." (Jeremiah 33:3 NIV)

Chapter 4
"You will keep in perfect peace all who trust in you, all whose thoughts are fixed on you!" (Isaiah 26:3 NLT)

"Then you will experience God's peace, which exceeds anything we can understand. His peace will guard your hearts and minds as you live in Christ Jesus." (Philippians 4:7 NLT)

"For God is not a God of confusion but of peace." (1 Corinthians 14:33 ESV)

"God is our refuge and strength, an ever-present help in trouble." (Psalm 46:1 NIV)

"Whenever my busy thoughts were out of control, the soothing comfort of your presence calmed me down and overwhelmed me with delight." (Psalm 94:19 TPT)

Chapter 5
"Move your heart closer and closer to God, and he will come even closer to you." (James 4:8 TPT)

"His purpose was for the nations to seek after God and perhaps feel their way toward him and find him—though he is not far from any one of us." (Acts 17:27 NLT)

"But God showed his great love for us by sending Christ to die for us while we were still sinners." (Romans 5:8 NLT)

"For God so loved the world, that he gave his only Son, that whoever believes in him should not perish but have eternal life. For God did not send his Son into the world to condemn the world, but in order that the world might be saved through him." (John 3:16–17 ESV)

"Yet look at you now! Everything is new! Although you were once distant and far away from God, now you have been brought delightfully close to him through the sacred blood of Jesus–you have actually been united to Christ!" (Ephesians 2:13 TPT)

"And he answered, 'You shall love the Lord your God with all your heart and with all your soul and with all your strength and with all your mind, and your neighbor as yourself.'" (Luke 10:27 ESV)

"And I am convinced that nothing can ever separate us from God's love. Neither death nor life, neither angels nor demons, neither our fears for today nor our worries about tomorrow—not even the powers of hell can separate us from God's love. No power in the sky above or in the earth below—indeed, nothing in all creation will ever be able to separate us from the love of God that is revealed in Christ Jesus our Lord." (Romans 8:38–39 NLT)

Chapter 6
"Be still, and know that I am God." (Psalm 46:10 ESV)

"In his hand is the life of every living thing and the breath of all mankind." (Job 12:10 ESV)

"Whenever my busy thoughts were out of control, the soothing comfort of your presence calmed me down and overwhelmed me with delight." (Psalm 94:19 TPT)

"His purpose was for the nations to seek after God and perhaps feel their way toward him and find him—though he is not far from any one of us." (Acts 17:27 NLT)

"Call to me and I will answer you, and will tell you great and hidden things that you have not known." (Jeremiah 33:3 ESV)

"You will keep in perfect peace all who trust in you, all whose thoughts are fixed on you!" (Isaiah 26:3 NLT)

"Move your heart closer and closer to God, and he will come even closer to you." (James 4:8 TPT)

"And I am convinced that nothing can ever separate us from God's love. Neither death nor life, neither angels nor demons, neither our fears for today nor our worries about tomorrow—not even the powers of hell can separate us from God's love. No power in the sky above or in the earth below—indeed, nothing in all creation will ever be able to separate us from the love of God that is revealed in Christ Jesus our Lord." (Romans 8:38–39 NLT)

Additional Reading

Learn to Breathe: The Surprising Path to a Transformed Life, by Dr. Jim Mindling

Two Dogs: Recognizing and Dealing With Our Two Conflicting Natures, by D. W. Fothergill

Acknowledgments

My husband, John, you continue to be my constant source of love and support. You encourage me to dream big and then tell me my dreams still aren't big enough. You have been my biggest cheerleader as I have worked on this book, and I wouldn't be where I am today without your love, patience, commitment, and friendship. I love you, babe.

Pastor Jim, your solid biblical teaching, wise counsel, and patience have impacted me more than you know as I have worked to rebuild my faith. Thank you for your insights and thoughtful critique of my rough draft and for helping me steward this message the Lord has given me.

Sammy Adebiyi, your excitement and support as I worked to get this book over the finish line encouraged me in so many ways. Thank you for reviewing my rough draft and for providing me with insightful feedback to help me make this book better than I could've made it on my own.

Sammie Davis-Dyson, that day we met for breakfast was timely! Hearing your story of writing and publishing your own book encouraged me to move forward with the publishing process of this one. Thank you for reviewing my early draft and nudging me to keep moving forward with this message.

Pastor Don, you faithfully walked with me during my darkest days of doubt without flinching and demonstrated to me the patient, vast love of the Father in a tangible way. My mind wandered back to our coffee shop conversations and your notes of encouragement many times as I worked on this manuscript.

About the Author

Christine Agostinelli has a fierce hunger to know and connect intimately with the heart of Jesus. In different seasons of her life this hunger has both driven her away from and drawn her back to her roots in the Christian faith. Now this hunger is what continues to drive her pursuit of a deep, genuine, and intimate connection with the heart of the One who knows and understands her best—Jesus Christ.

Unsatisfied and angry at the age of twenty-five, Christine left the Christian faith she had been raised with in search of something that would satisfy her growing hunger for *more*. After eight long years and many long struggles with her beliefs, she found herself curiously drawn back to the faith she had left and had once promised herself she would never return to.

It is now her joy and passion to share with others what she has learned while walking through dark days of doubt and beautiful days of redemption in her quest to finally find a faith that truly satisfies.

Christine resides near the shores of Lake Erie in Northern Ohio with her husband, John, and their two children.

You can read more about her story on her blog at:
www.ChristineAgostinelli.com

Or follow her on facebook (@ChristineAgostinelli) or Instagram (@Christine_Agostinelli)